I0753039

ANIMALS

Rebecca Woodbury, Ph.D., M.Ed.

Gravitas Publications Inc.

Animals

Illustrations: Janet Moneymaker

Animals (hardcover)
ISBN 978-1-953542-49-6

Published by Gravitas Publications Inc.
Imprint: Real Science-4-Kids
www.gravitaspublications.com
www.realscience4kids.com

Photo credits: Cover & Title Page: By Eric Isselée, AdobeStock; Above, By kuritafsheen, AdobeStock; P.3. By kozorog, AdobeStock; P.5. By Leka, AdobeStock; P.6. By Happy monkey; P.7. By an, AdobeStock; P.9. By DBA, AdobeStock; P.10-11. By Eric Isselée, AdobeStock; P.12. By Leoniek, AdobeStock; P.13. By janstria, AdobeStock; P.14. By Silviu, AdobeStock; P.15. By vlad61_61, AdobeStock; P.16. By Vidu Gunaratna, AdobeStock; P.17. By kuritafsheen, AdobeStock; P.18. By sweetlaniko, AdobeStock; P.19. By dpep, AdobeStock; P.20. By New Africa, AdobeStock; P.21. By Alexey Kuznetsov, AdobeStock

There are many kinds of animals.

Animals look different from each other.

Some animals have fur.

Some animals have scales.

Some animals have wings.

Animals have different

numbers of legs.

Animals live everywhere!

Some animals live in dirt.

Some animals live on top of lakes.

Some animals live in the ocean.

Some animals live in trees.

Some animals live in houses.

Other animals build their own houses.

How many different animals

can you see?

How to say science words

animal (AA-nuh-muhl)

fur (FUHR)

leg (LEG)

ocean (OH-shuhn)

scale (SKAYL)

science (SIY-ens)

wing (WING)

www.ingramcontent.com/pod-product-compliance
Lightning Source LLC
LaVergne TN
LVHW060602110826
845154LV00003B/21
* 9 7 8 1 9 5 3 5 4 2 4 9 6 *